A FATHER'S GUIDE TO RAISING DAUGHTERS

HOW TO BOOST HER SELF-ESTEEM, SELF-IMAGE AND SELF-RESPECT

Michael T. Wilkinson

Kindermill Publishing

DuPont, Washington

Cover designed by: Publishmybook.today

Published in the United States of America

ISBN-13: 9781516830084

ISBN-10: 1516830083

PRAISE FOR A FATHER'S GUIDE TO RAISING DAUGHTERS

"I am beyond happy to see this type of 'rubber meets the road' coaching in printed form. Dads - do yourself and your daughters a huge favor - buy this book!" - **Megan C. Scott**, author, Low Carb Egg Cookbook

"For fathers who are raising daughters, and are looking for a down-to-earth, practical and inspirational source material based on real accounts of how to connect with daughters, this is the book you want." - **Scott Allan**, author, Rejection Reset

"Beautifully written - a must read for any parent! Thoughtful, respectful and tremendously encouraging and understanding. Dads who want to be even 'better dads' will become the ultimate awesome dad after reading this!! And for mums, Father's Guide to Raising

Daughters is very insightful. Love it!" - **Coral Emerson**, Australia, Office Manager in Tourism

"There is so much to learn from this book! Wilkinson addresses real-life issues here and shares the best advice out there for raising a confident, smart, and kind girl. If you feel lost with how to show your daughter how much you love her, read this book." - **Krista Brubaker**, author, Dare to Resonate

"A great book for fathers to help raise their daughters to be Great people. This is one of the best books ever written for fathers. All fathers should get this book to take home with them from the hospital when their daughter is born." - **Sandy Schultz**, author, Hourglass Fitness Over 50

"Michael's book is a treasure for dads and daughters. As a father of girls, I could relate to everything he wrote." - **David Woody**, author, Active Prayers for Busy Families

"As a father of 2 girls, I was extremely impressed with this book and I would recommend it to anyone who wants to raise a happy, confident, and loving daughter." - **Sean Sumner**, author, Neck Check: Chronic Neck Pain Relief Once and For All

"This is a great one. Michael does such a great job of delving deep into the things you are responsible for as a dad." - **Steve Windsor**, author, Nine Day Novel – Authorphobia

TABLE OF CONTENTS

Introduction

What should you be teaching your daughter right now? What can you do for her now that will make a difference in her life later?

If you're like most dads, then you probably love your daughter as much as the other dads love theirs. Maybe you've wondered whether you're preparing your daughter for that day when she finally stops holding your hand and no longer needs to ask your permission.

Maybe she's already there. I should know because I have two of my own, and one is approaching that age. Today, she's daddy's little girl, but tomorrow she'll be all grown up.

With daughters, you worry. You worry about how boys will treat them or how to protect them from harm. You may even worry where to stash your baseball bat so you can whip that baby out when that first boy comes knocking on your door. (I'm kidding about that last one.)

How are you preparing your daughter?

Here's the thing.

The world will try hard to dismantle any positive messages we give our daughters. So it's important our messages boost their self-esteem, self-image, and self-respect as much as possible. Imagine how much better your daughter's life could be if you taught her the life lessons found in this book. Lessons that:

1) Give her the confidence to get back up and try again after her fourth, fifth, and sixth falls while learning to rollerblade.

2) Give her enough self-respect to refuse to reward a boy's charm by sexting naked images of herself from her smartphone.

3) Give her a positive self-image to recognize her worth after her so-called friends shun her because of how she looks or what she wears.

How many girls receive that type of fatherly advice these days? How many girls fail to recognize their value and seek validation from sleazy jerks or fake friends who try to take advantage of them?

I don't know about you, but I won't allow that to happen to my girls. Dads like us don't just want to think our girls will do better, we want to know it. We can't hold their hands forever. Eventually, they'll let go.

So let's show them how to pick themselves up whenever life knocks them down. If you're finding that easier said than done—like I did—then fortunately there's a way to fix it.

I discovered what other dads were doing that worked for them. I also listened to women tell their childhood stories about their dads. Then, something happened.

I started to see a pattern. Every success story involved a father instilling life-long lessons and values into his daughters that would prepare them for the future.

Before I reveal what that is, I want you to know something about me. As the father of two girls and a parent for over 12 years, I've been through the trenches, failing and succeeding at being a father.

Perhaps you and I have similar dreams for our girls—that they have happy, healthy, and successful lives. We work hard every day to make sure we're giving them the love and support they'll need before they leave the nest. That's why I've written down what's been working for me, just for you.

What you'll discover in this book

In this book, you'll discover what many dads like you are doing right now in the lives of their daughters.

Plus, you'll see expert advice on what to do, so you'll have peace of mind you're doing the right thing, too.

Finally, you'll read stories of several women who reveal their childhood experiences growing up with or without a father and how this has affected their lives.

I'll also reveal my personal successes and failures, so you can avoid what I did wrong and copy what I did right.

This book is not a case study in the field of psychology, although I reference certain psychological concepts. In addition to suggesting ways to boost your daughter's self-esteem, self-image, and self-respect, themes in this book include:

1) overcoming adversity

2) respecting herself and others

3) persevering through difficult times

4) building self-confidence

Why you should read this book

If you're like me and most dads, then you're probably not the perfect father you see on TV. And that's okay because that guy stinks anyway. He's fake.

In the real world, we do the best we can. My hope is to share my knowledge with you. This is my reason why I wrote this book.

So what should a father teach his daughter by age, 7, 11, or 16 so that when she turns 22, she'll be ready to take on the world?

You've heard it before—teach her to be kind and sweet; tell her to never kiss on the first date.

But you already know smart dads go beyond that, junk.

So, what do you say during those adolescent years that will prepare her for the future? What should you be teaching your daughter right now?

In this book, you'll learn life-changing lessons that will reveal things like:

1) The truth about fatherhood no one ever talks about until now.

2) How you can help your daughter gain self-respect almost overnight.

3) How to get your daughter to want to listen to you over and over again.

4) And much more!

As you read through this book, you'll see patterns emerge as men and women from around the world share their stories.

You'll meet people like:

1) Liz whose dad saved her life in a car crash years before it even happened

2) Julie whose struggle with her father's alcoholism still affects her decades later

3) Sean who spends quality time with his daughter using a cell phone

4) Mikal whose teenage daughter made a surprising decision after he and his wife filed for bankruptcy

5) And many others

You may already know many of the principles in this book, and if so, that's great. But ask yourself: Am I already teaching my daughter these principles on a regular basis through my words and actions?

In his book, The Success Principles, Jack Canfield asserts, "Principles only work if you work the principles." I happen to agree. So, I recommend you highlight or bookmark passages in this book you want to remember, share, or tweet later.

And remember to add whatever you discover in this book to whatever you're already doing. Do it for your daughter's sake. The more you know, the further she'll go.

If you don't teach her, you fail her.

I'm not saying you need become her cheerleader. What I'm saying is at some point in your daughter's life—and throughout her childhood—someone is going to tell her, "You're awesome!"

"I believe in you!"

"Great job!

You're beautiful!"

"You can do it!"

But, there will always be someone who says, "You stink!"

"You're stupid!"

"You're fat!

You're ugly!"

And she'll believe them because that's what kids do. They believe what people say. So it's up to us to make sure she hears the right message. We have to not only decide which words we want our daughters to hear, but also decide to be the first ones to say them.

Now, if you believe this book will turn your little tomboy into a pedestal princess or turn your darling daughter into the next Oprah Winfrey, then this book is not for you.

This book is about boosting your daughter's self-esteem so she can make the right choices when you're no longer holding her hand to cross the street.

Some dads don't teach their daughters these lessons because these lessons weren't taught to them by their parents.

They can't show what they don't know.

Just imagine all the girls who grow up without their father's advice. Do any of them live nearby? Are any of them related to you? Do they have low self-esteem? Do they respect themselves and others around them? Are they confident enough to know they don't need a man to take care of them when they get older?

Now imagine your daughter in the future. You've given her all the tools she'll need to be successful when she grows up. You've taught her to respect herself as well as the people around her. You've taught her to look in the mirror and see a beautiful young lady staring back. Height and dress size have no stronghold over how she feels about herself.

You've taught her that she is capable and worthy of doing anything in this world she wants to do. Finally, imagine your daughter thanking you years from now because you showed interest in her by reading and implementing the ideas found in this book.

I know every family is different. But, if you follow the advice in this book, you will not only improve your daughter's life, but also become a better parent because of it. If you add these lessons to your parenting style, then they will have a positive impact on your daughter's future. Don't you want your girls to have that advantage?

What you should do next

Don't be the dad who misses out on an opportunity by procrastinating and forgetting all about it. Instead, be the dad who takes action, the dad that others want to be like. Start by reading this book.

Think of where you are and where you want to be. You're her parent but are you her role model, too? I can show you the path, you just have to walk it. You don't need to be perfect. You just need to be present.

In chapter one, I want to address your frustrations if you're still having doubts about raising a daughter. Plus, I'm going to tell you how you can fix it starting today(Now if you've gotten over your frustration, you can skip ahead to the chapter after next.). Turn the page, and I'll tell you what WWE pro wrestler, Kane, a bunch of balloons, and two little girls have in common.

Discover the one thing about fatherhood that no one ever talks about. Turn the page to find out more.

CHAPTER 1

The One Truth about Fatherhood No One Tells You

Were you expecting a boy?

If so, then you'll want to read this chapter where you'll find out something that most people believe only affects women and what you can do to fix it. Every father who falls into this category believes one common lie: that he is alone.

Before I discovered this one thing, I thought I was alone, too. Then, I discovered the truth. To fully understand what I mean, allow me to tell you my story.

Unfulfilled expectations

That night, I drove to the hospital like I was behind the wheel of a getaway car. When we arrived, I felt my heart pounding in my ears. As I placed my wife in a wheelchair, I saw her face wrench in agony.

The baby was coming.

Panic and excitement coursed through me as I sprinted through the halls. The attendant leading the way was just as panicked. Maybe this was his first baby, too.

There was just one problem, though. Our baby wasn't born right away. I knew then it was going to be a long labor for my wife. But thank God for epidurals. That drug saved her from a lot of pain.

Twelve hours later, my wife gave birth the next morning. I remember seeing the tip of the baby's head and asking myself, "Is it a boy?"

Weeks earlier, my wife and I were sure we were having a boy. We were so sure that, during the ultrasound, instead of learning the baby's sex, we decided we wanted to be "surprised."

After my wife had delivered, the midwife held the baby up, exclaiming, "Surprise! It's a girl." Oops!

Daniella arrived one snowy winter's morning in February 2002.

Having a girl when you expected a boy

If you're like me, then you probably felt a little surprised, maybe even a little disappointed. Though I was overjoyed—my daughter was born, and I embraced my new role as a dad—I didn't have a clue how to raise her. I was scared I'd make a mistake; that I'd screw up.

At the time, I didn't know these feelings were normal.

They are normal for you, too. You're not frustrated in your daughter. You're frustrated because you expected a son and it didn't happen. You wanted a little boy to watch movies with you, to hunt, to hang out at games, to coach in Little League.

You knew all along that having a girl was a possibility, but for whatever reason, you never thought it would actually happen. Never. And you feel like you missed your opportunity to continue the family name. You felt like you failed.

Perhaps, you felt so angry and frustrated, you wanted to leave.

If you felt anything like this, then you're not wrong. It turns out—it's normal. And what you're feeling has a name.

It's called gender disappointment.

It's a condition usually associated with new mothers, but it can affect news dads, too. It doesn't affect every new father, but it does affect more than you know. Most guys rarely acknowledge how they feel, partly because men normally don't discuss their feelings openly.

Many forums, support groups, and resources exist to help women deal with their disappointment. We, on the other hand, don't experience the same level of emotional support as women.

Feeling disappointed is normal

You're not a jerk for feeling depressed, especially when you see another father with his son doing the things you dreamed of doing.

Perhaps, you felt cheated. Maybe you have brothers, and you brothers had boys, and your brothers-in-law had boys. So naturally, you thought you'd have one, too.

Fortunately, these feelings are temporary. Most fathers overcome them immediately as I did. But what happens when you can't get over your disappointment?

Here are several things you can do to deal with gender disappointment.

5 Ways to Beat Gender Disappointment[1]

In her article, Secretly Sad: Overcoming Gender Disappointment, on babble.com, Andrea Elovson suggests several ways to deal with this issue:

1. Talk about how you feel.

Talking about our feelings is not something men typically do. But sometimes we need to talk to someone that we not only trust but also someone who has earned the right to hear what we have to say.

This person needs to be someone who won't judge you or hate you for being honest. This person needs to able to hear the cold hard truth—that you may have been a little disappointed when you found out you were having a girl.

Remember, your disappointment is temporary, so you don't want to tell someone who may hold a grudge long after you've gotten over your disappointment.

2. Give yourself time to grieve.

Yes, that's right. Grieve. You'll need to give yourself time to feel the disappointment and allow yourself time to get over it before you can move past these feelings. Bottling up these feeling and not dealing with them will only cause you to exhibit them in undesirable ways.

For example, you may snap in anger at people you love. You may have a short temper with friends and co-workers. You may even get angry at the smallest things like someone beating you to a parking space or standing in line at a coffee shop too long. You may become emotionally withdrawn, not speaking at all to your family.

3. Understand what you're experiencing.

Understand that what you're feeling is not a disappointment in your daughter but frustration due to the expectation of a son. This unfulfilled expectation occurred when you expect one result and get another. For example, you expected to have a son but instead, you got a daughter. Therefore, you should resolve to stop feeling guilty about being disappointed.

4. Shout it out.

If telling a friend doesn't work for you, then let your frustration out some other way. Air your feelings out in the open by acknowledging them out loud. Sit in your car or somewhere safe from prying ears and yell. Deal with how you're feeling. Sitting on your feelings and hoping they will disappear will only make it worse.

5. Challenge your assumptions about having a girl versus a boy

Write down what you thought you might have gained by having a son. Then challenge those assumptions to see if they are valid. For example, you may write down the following:

1) "Boys like the kind of movies I like." The reality is girls do too. According to the Motion Picture Association of America, women make up 50% of all moviegoers. Chances are in your favor that your daughter will want to see the Avengers movie, like my daughter, when she's old enough.

2) "Boys do things with their dads that wives and daughters don't." I get that. But there are so many things you can do with your daughter. You just need to suspend your disbelief and imagine the possibilities.

Or you can just Google it. You'll find women hiking, biking, boxing, hunting, shooting, camping, farming, lifting, playing all sports (yes, they play football, too), racing, diving, and flying. I think you get my point. Girls do it all. Why would your daughter be any different?

What will you have in common with your daughter?

I get it. You can't stand tea parties and Barbie dolls.

But you can do just about everything with a daughter that you can with a son. It's not the same, but it's just as fun. Let go of your limiting beliefs or you'll miss out on the greatest experience of your life: being a dad to a beautiful little girl.

What I have in common with my girls

If you're like most dads, then you probably already know that you can have a lot of fun with daughters. For instance, my girls and I play balloon wars. Yes, I said it: we have a war with the balloons. And those balloons always lose.

See, every birthday, I blow up a lot of balloons. Then we move the furniture around to clear a space in the living room. (You can do this outside, too. But since my girls were winter babies, we play indoors during their birthdays.) Then the fun begins.

If you're a WWE fan, imagine you're Kane coming into the ring. You raise your arms and lower them as the lights go out. At the same time, fire shoots out into the air from the turnbuckles. Oh, yeah.

"Welcome to the next battle of BALLOON WAAAAAAARS!!!! (Cue the fake crowd noise.) Are you ready?" I ask.

"YEAH!"

"You!" I pronounce, pointing to the little one. "Are you ready?"

"YEAH, DADDY."

"READY! SET!! GO!!!"

Each girl darts out from her corner with pen in hand and pounces on the nearest balloon.

POP! POP … POP!

There're lots of screaming and laughing and balloon guts everywhere. And it's loads of fun for them. It's something we all look forward to.

You definitely don't need to have sons to be happy. You just need to make memories—lots of them.

You can copy that if you want. You can even draw evil faces on the balloons to make it more fun. Play the Game of Thrones theme song while you're at it. In fact, if you do, record a video of it for me on your phone and email it to me. I'd love to see it.

What to do now?

I'll admit I felt a little disappointed at first because I was expecting a boy. But that feeling lasted about 5 seconds because I was overjoyed that I had become a father. And I loved my daughter even before she was born.

You have an excellent addition to your family and a great opportunity to raise a little daughter into a blossoming young woman. In many cases, how your daughter develops, in terms of her interests, personality, and attitude are heavily influenced by your presence, relationship, and interaction with them on a continuous and consistent basis.

If you still have doubts, then you have a choice: become the great dad she loves or become the man she hates. Remember—the reason you're reading this book is to build her up, not tear her apart.

Download your free quick and easy cheat sheet of the five ways to deal with gender disappointment at www.raisingyourdaughter.com/gender.

What's next?

In the next chapter, you discover how to boost your daughter's confidence. How do you do that? And is what you're doing to boost her confidence working for her? Find out ways to help you out.

CHAPTER 2

What You Should Know about her Self-Esteem (And How You Can Boost It)

Do you know if your daughter lacks confidence? If so, what happened in her life that caused her to doubt her looks, or her body or her other qualities? Worse, how long has it been going on?

After reading this chapter, you'll be able to recognize when your daughter may be feeling a lack of confidence. And you'll know how to handle it. Let's discuss what you can do to help her improve her self-confidence right now.

You do want to build her up, right?

Getting our daughters to feel confident seems harder to do nowadays, especially when tanned bikini-clad bodies with 0% body fat, blonde hair, and eyes like blue pearls adorn almost every magazine cover.

Celebrities and supermodels have become the standard bearers of beauty now more than ever. Spot them in TV ads or popping up on computer screens and smartphones.

They're everywhere. Our society seems to celebrate this ideal image of beauty while ignoring anyone who doesn't appear to measure up. And of course, most men love that stuff. We're men, right? Raise your hand if you were turned on by some eye-popping, jaw-dropping, hot sexy young babe, today?

But what about your daughter?

She's seen those images, too. What do you think is going through her head right now? How does she feel when she sees those images?

Have you seen her face when she's watching commercials on TV, movies or on social media that display these images day after day? Have you ever talked to her about what she's seeing?

If you're like most dads, then you're probably already thinking about how to protect your daughter from negative thoughts about her body image that are eating away at her self-esteem.

So, how do you do that?

You'll want to start by boosting her confidence. This will allow her to resist those thoughts and see herself as a unique, intelligent, beautiful, and gifted young lady—the same way you see her every day.

Of course, without confidence your daughter (and mine) will continue to have self-doubt. She'll feel ugly, dull, or unattractive. She'll slouch and cast her eyes downward.

She'll begin to make excuses or feel the need to defend herself every time someone expresses an opinion different from hers.

She'll feel pressure to be perfect like those airbrushed wafer thin vixens on magazine covers.

She'll project her lack of confidence in how she speaks and dresses.

Worse, if she is old enough to date, she'll listen to the first jerk that comes along and makes her feel special or tells her she's pretty.

But there's a solution.

What can you do to fix it?

First of all, understand there is no magic pill or instant cure. Instead, you should take the time to figure out what works best for you and your daughter. Below, I give you ten ways to help you build your daughter's confidence.

10 Ways to Boost Your Daughter's Confidence

1. Make your daughter media literate.

If you watch TV or movies or use the Internet, then you probably realize how often our minds are flooded with thousands of images of the perfect body, the perfect eyes, the perfect hair, or whatever.

And you may also realize how often your daughter is exposed to these images too.

So what can you do about it?

Of course, you can limit her time in front of the TV. Take away the smartphone if she's old enough to have one. Or you could forbid her to use the Internet. Or you could restrict her to watching only G-rated movies.

But those options aren't really as practical these days as they used to be, especially since technology places these images everywhere.

So, again, what can you do?

Well, you'll want to have an honest conversation with your daughter and explain that these images are fake. I don't mean that the people in these pictures are fake plastic-looking robots.

I mean you need to explain to your daughter that images of people she sees in media are designed for three purposes—to entertain, to inform, or to get you to buy.

Remind her that most people don't go about their day looking flawless like the girls on America's Next Top Model (I don't watch that show. I'm just making a point.)

She shouldn't compare herself to these images, right? The same goes for the Kardashians or MTV or BET or your favorite reality TV show.

Sometimes, I forget to let my girls know this or assume that they already get it. But, after I see their faces and watch their eyes glaze over the supposedly age-appropriate images on TV after I change the channel, I explain to them how they should interpret what they're seeing. I always start by saying, "You know that's not real, right?"

2. Be careful of the kind of magazines you leave around the house.

The same thing goes for magazines as it does for images on television and online. You may be thinking I'm referring to porn or gentlemen's magazines, yes? But those are too obvious. Actually, I'm referring to something less conspicuous.

Fitness, beauty and even some teen magazines are worthy sources of information and entertainment. But, if you have a ton of magazines with airbrushed images of gorgeous bikini models gracing the covers, chances are your daughter has seen them. She may have even purchased some of them. And now she may feel the urge to compare herself to them as well.

So how often should you have a conversation about these things? You should have them as often as necessary. Don't wait until your daughter starts to feel like she doesn't measure up. Start now.

Get those self-limiting thoughts about her appearance out of her head as early as possible, so when the day comes and you're not there ready to explain why she doesn't look like the half-naked vixen on the cover of some magazine, she'll already know that it's just an illusion.

3. Don't treat her like a damsel in distress.

Have you seen the Disney movie Frozen? If you have a young daughter, then maybe you've seen it once or twice. If you're like me, though, you've seen it a million times.

Like many animated films, this one tells a story of a beautiful young maiden who must maneuver her way out of danger while singing.

But, the difference between Princess Ana in this film and other Disney princesses is that Ana doesn't need to be saved. Yes, she needs help, but she doesn't need to be rescued by a dashing young prince. She's actually the heroine.

Like Ana, your daughter isn't some damsel in distress either.

Is it possible that parents sometimes treat their daughters like fragile little porcelain dolls? The truth is our girls are tougher than we realize. Treating them like victims will only cause them to act like victims.

They will become less resilient to adversity and cower at every obstacle, always waiting for a man to rush in and save the day. You don't want that to happen. Am I right?

Perhaps, you want your daughter to be more like the heroine and less like the victim. I'm not saying treat her like a boy. Just don't treat her like glass.

In other words, encourage her to solve her own problems before you intervene.

Decide what skills your daughter might ask a man to perform. Then, teach her that skill.

Empower her to rescue herself.

For example, if she's old enough, teach your daughter to paint a room, mow the lawn, wash the car or change a flat tire.

Don't limit yourself to these ideas.

Find something age-appropriate for your daughter. What could you teach her now that will help her in the future?

4. Kill negative thoughts.[2]

If you're anything like me, then you've probably heard other people talk about the power of positive thinking. I get it. You definitely want to carry a positive mindset throughout your day. More importantly, you want your daughter to have one too. But it's not enough to have her just think of rainbows and butterflies all day long.

To build her confidence, you've got to teach her to squash those negative thoughts that seem to creep up out of nowhere. If she doesn't kill those critters, they will feed on her self-esteem like vermin.

So what do you do?

First, if you experience negative self-talk, then you need to learn how to stop it yourself. You can't teach what you don't know. Whenever negative self-talk creeps into your mind, you need to recognize it, stop it, and then replace it with positive thoughts.

Some people do this by verbally telling themselves that the negative thought is not true. Whenever Leo Babauta gets negative thoughts, he imagines himself swatting them down like a bug and stomping on them. Squish! Discover more of what Leo does to boost confidence on his blog, ZenHabits.net

Find out what works for you, and then teach it to your daughter. Whenever she feels she'll never pass math test or make new friends, she'll need to know what to do in order to defeat the negative self-talk.

5. Act positively.[3]

Sometimes, the worst thing you can do in a situation is overreact. Children are hardwired to mirror our behavior, especially when it comes to how we react. I've seen this with my older daughter Dani, and I see it today with my younger daughter Kayla.

You see, at 5 years old, Kayla, used to wet the bed. It was perfectly normal for her age. We checked. But she still felt embarrassed and ashamed when it happened. Every time it happened though, my wife or I would have to strip the bed, wash the sheets, remake the bed with fresh linen, and pray it didn't happen again.

I used to get angry about it, and I let it show. I saw the shame and sadness in her face. I put it there. It was the worst feeling in the world.

What I've learned to do instead was to act positively. I didn't put on a façade and act like nothing happened. Instead, I didn't yell or frown or give her the silent treatment.

I'm telling you this because I don't want you to make the same mistake I made. I'm not just referring to bed-wetting. I'm referring to any situation where your daughter makes a mistake or has no control over the outcome. (For example, she wasn't born a boy. If this is still a problem for you, I suggest you read chapter one.)

I've learned to tell her the truth and remind her that everything is okay. I smile because I want her to know that this too shall pass. I remain calm and act positively.

6. Be kind.

This one sounds too obvious. But if we don't consciously make it a habit to be kind and loving to our daughters, then we run the risk of coming across as jerks.

Of course, that's not our intent. But the mistake some fathers make is they assume their daughters know how they feel or what they mean.

I make a conscious effort to be kind to my daughters. Why? I do this because, over the years, I've come to realize that sometimes I can be a little, well … mean. I don't do it intentionally.

I think it's just a guy thing. I sometimes get a little excited during a football game on television or otherwise preoccupied in my man cave doing my thing. In the past, my reaction to them disturbing me may have been a little less than kind. Has that ever happened to you?

Kindness is a no-brainer. But it's a virtue we fail to think about during fourth quarter of the Super Bowl when your team tosses a pick at the goal line instead of running the ball for a touchdown.

That's why you shouldn't take being kind for granted like I did. Instead, remember to be understanding and helpful to your daughter. Slip-ups will occur. Just recognize your slip-ups and try again with the kindness.

7. Stand straight.[4]

Encourage your daughter to stand straight and not slouch. Yes, I know this seems lame, but bear with me. You see, standing up straight makes you feel more confident and, as a result, causes you to project confidence.

Askmen.com lists standing up straight as one of the ten ways to project confidence with body language. Getting your daughter to straighten up will boost her confidence as well. And if this is good for guys, it's definitely right for your daughter.

This means you have to do it too. Your daughter will follow your lead on this. If she sees you doing it, she is more likely to imitate your actions. Remember, children don't just do what we say, they do what they see. So be mindful of what you're doing because your daughter will emulate that.

8. Encourage her.

Sometimes we forget that our daughters need to hear an encouraging word from us. Thinking silently to ourselves about how much we believe in our girls is not enough. We need to say it to them.

The words you say don't have to be a long, drawn-out monolog about how much you believe in her potential. You just have to be there to lift her up when she doubts herself.

You don't lie or make stuff up.

You just want her to realize that you believe in her and that you want her to believe in herself too.

Remember, you're building her confidence, not inflating her ego. Tell her, "You can do it," "I believe in you," or "You got this." Say something that reassures your daughter that she can achieve success.

Ask yourself: What have I said to my daughter to encourage her today?

9. Project a proper appearance.

This goes without saying. But I thought I'd mention it because the way you dress and groom yourself is important.

My mother once told me what you wear and how you look will determine how people react to you and will, therefore, affect your confidence. She told me this when I was much younger. I didn't agree with her then, but by the time I became a teenager, I realized she was right.

Grooming and the way you dress are important. Please don't take this to mean you have to buy expensive outfits and $300 hairdos for your daughter. What I'm saying is she'll want to feel good about her appearance, especially around other people.

One side note: You don't want to focus your confidence-building efforts on how she looks. That would be an epic failure. It would cause her to feel confident only when she's being complimented on her appearance. You'll want to avoid that.

Your daughter is much more than a pretty face and a beautiful dress. If you want other people to acknowledge her for who she is and not just how she looks, then you must acknowledge it too.

10. Watch what you say and how you say it.

Years ago, a friend told me, "It's not what you say; it's how you say it."

Sometimes I forget what I say and how I say it affects my daughters. Because tough guys like us don't often cry, I have to remind myself that my first instinct to question my daughter about why she is crying may be inappropriate.

Instead, it's actually better to empathize with how she's feeling instead of questioning why she's feeling a certain way. That doesn't mean I need to baby her or give in to every teardrop.

It simply means that I need to let her know I understand and that crying is normal. It just means—I need to watch what I say and how I say it.

What to do now?

The key to boosting your daughter's confidence is to help her feel good about herself. What can you say to her to make her smile? How can you compliment her efforts? Tell her what you admire about something she's done. Think about what you can say that will brighten her day and boost her confidence.

Here's a reminder:

1) Tell her the truth about the media

2) Treat her like a heroine

3) Encourage her with your words and actions

4) Help her project a proper appearance

5) If you'd like a free one-page guide listing all 10 ways to boost your daughter's confidence, you can find it at: www.raisingyourdaughter.com/confidence.

What's next?

Respect your efforts, respect yourself. Self-respect leads to self-discipline. When you have both firmly under your belt, that's real power. - Clint Eastwood

How does this quote fit into helping you help your daughter? Next you'll find out how this relates to building your daughter's self-esteem. You'll also discover how a story about the coffee house barista, an early morning school drop-off, and an Easter egg hunt are tied together. Hint: it's probably not what you think.

CHAPTER 3

How To Help Your Daughter Gain Self-Respect Starting Today

Did you know the easiest way to get your daughter to rebel is to criticize her every decision, undermine her in front of her peers, and say no to her every request?

This is a foolproof way of losing her respect, much less keeping it.

So what should you do instead? And how can you teach her to respect herself and others even when those others may not be showing her respect?

What I'm about to share is important because, without this knowledge, your daughter could someday doubt herself or develop an inability to earn the respect of others unless you do something about it.

What happens to girls' self-respect?

Lorna Blumen, co-creator of "Girls' Respect Groups," an after-school program for middle school girls, suggests that girls' self-esteem plummets around age 10, so it is imperative you intervene now to prevent that from happening.

So, what should you do to teach your daughter about respect? What can you do to help your daughter right now?

In the pages that follow, you'll find several ways you can start boosting your daughter's self-respect today.

I believe dads like us want to raise our daughters' levels of self-respect and prevent trolls from knocking it down.

I'll share exactly what dads like us have done to build their daughters up. Plus, you'll discover tools to help you instill this life-long virtue in your daughter's life. But first, I want to share what happened to my daughter and me the other day.

How to show respect for others?

"Move!" she screamed.

That word was the match that lit my fuse. I was about to get into a heated argument with another parent who was dropping off her son at school. Early morning rush hour was not the time to get in my way when I'm dropping off my daughter at school.

My jaw clenched. My eyes boiled. My face turned blood red. And my fist was ready to fly. But I stayed calm.

But, why?

Minutes earlier, I saw that same woman's car preparing to leave a parking spot right across the street from the front door of the school. I wanted it. It was mine. But she decided to sit and wait.

Typical.

I was in a hurry, so I drove my SUV into the empty spot in front of hers. Then, she pulled her car out behind mine, preventing me from backing into my parking spot.

She wanted me to drive away. But I would have lost the parking space. I wanted her to go around, but she didn't wish to drive into the opposing lane.

"Move, please!" she yelled out again.

I wanted to honk my horn and bark her head off, but then I looked in the rearview mirror at my little

Mikayla in the backseat. What I did next may surprise you.

Before I tell you what happened next, let me give you several techniques dads use to help boost their daughters' self-respect.

6 Tricks to Develop Self-Respect In Your Daughter Without Her Knowing[5]

In her article, Teaching Kids Self-Respect Early Is Crucial, Lorna Brumen lists several ideas to help develop self-respect in children. By employing these simple techniques over time, you can develop your daughter's self-respect and her respect for others without her even knowing (unless you spill the beans).

1. Set an example by showing her how to respect others.

Have you ever heard the expression, "Show 'em what right looks like"?

Possibly, the most important thing to remember when teaching your daughter about respect is that she will model you. She will observe you and copy everything you do.

So if you want her to respect herself and respect other people including their property, then consider showing her what the right way to respect someone looks like. Set an example for her to follow.

She needs to see you respecting her mother. She needs to see you respect the woman behind the counter at the coffee shop. She needs to see you respect the woman at the checkout counter.

She even needs to see you respect the woman leaving the parking space (and screaming at you) after dropping off her son at school.

2. Show respect for yourself.

The easiest way to demonstrate self-respect is to speak positively about yourself even when you make a mistake. Speaking negatively about yourself in front of your daughter may cause her to do the same whenever she makes a mistake.

Sure, mistakes will happen. You'll forget to put gas in the car or you'll miss paying your credit card bill by the due date. You may even fall behind on your mortgage. Instead of using harsh language to criticize yourself in front of your daughter, encourage yourself by saying something positive like, "That didn't go so well. But I'm going to do better next time." Whatever it is you say, make sure it's positive and that she hears you say it.

3. Avoid gossip.

Showing respect for others involves something that many people—men included—sometimes have a hard time avoiding. That thing is gossip. Should dads like us teach our daughters to do that?

49

If we did, then we'd risk training them to be disrespectful. Worse, when people show disrespect for others, they invite other people to disrespect them in return. If she sees you gossiping, she'll feel okay about doing it too.

4. Avoid the silent treatment.

This one is tough for dads like me. But I always try to remember that my silence can cause more harm than good. One never knows how badly ignoring a child can affect her self-esteem.

So I avoid it. Instead, whenever I'm not in the mood to talk, I let my daughters know that now isn't the right time, and I will talk with them later. At least they won't feel like I'm shutting them out.

And that point brings me to my next one.

5. Treat your daughter with respect, even when you're angry or disappointed in her.

I'll admit it—sometimes I lose my temper. I've learned the hard way to avoid allowing my anger to speak for me. I try not to let my anger cause me to say something I'll regret later. Even if you don't have a bad temper, you'll want to make a conscious effort as well to treat your daughter with respect even when she messes up.

Now, that's an easy thing to say. But, what do you do when you lose control? How are you supposed to deal with that situation? Sometimes, anger will pour out of you like an open fire hydrant in August. It happens.

I still get angry. Sometimes, I get angry a lot. So, when I feel a nuclear meltdown coming on, I count to 10, I ask my wife to intervene or I tell my daughters we'll discuss it later, then I walk away. In other words, I give myself time to cool off.

What do you do when you get angry? Think about that question for a moment. Is what you're doing working? If not, try my tips above to help you. Just remember that becoming angry is normal. It will happen to the best of us. So, work to be mindful of the things that trigger your anger so you can avoid them.

6. Teach her empathy.

Empathy is possibly the best way to show respect for another human being. Jim Stovall, speaker and author of the novel The Ultimate Gift, stated, "When we all help one another, everybody wins."

Are girls naturally empathetic? Perhaps they are, but remember your daughter will model your behavior too. Therefore, you may want to teach her to see things from the other person's perspective.

Case Study One

David is a preacher from Charleston, South Carolina. He has three daughters, his own two, Brooks, 17 and

51

Blair, 14, and his stepdaughter Sarah, 13. Every day, he tries to instill in them the idea that nobody's perfect and that everyone is fallible.

"What's wrong with Sarah?" asked Brooks.

David explained that Sara was very upset because some obnoxious girl invited herself to hang out with Sarah and her friends at Starbucks before school one morning.

"This girl's trying to separate me from my friends," Sarah lamented.

David explained the situation about this girl to his eldest daughter Brooks.

"Does this girl have any other friends?" Brooks asked. "Does she have anybody else to hang out with?"

That was her first response—empathy.

David says he tries to teach his children that everybody's human and to see the world from their points of view. He thinks they get it.

"Brooks and Blair have seen me (and their mother) treat people and talk about (and to) people in a certain way," he said. "They've learned from our example."

David's step-daughter Sarah, who is the youngest girl, is still watching and learning from her older step-sisters. She'll learn over time.

Case Study Two

In another case study, Sean, a physical therapist from California talks about witnessing his daughter during a family gathering at his home one Easter. This is Sean explaining here:

"My older daughter, Emma, was playing with some other kids that were having a difficult time keeping up with her. She's a little bit tall and quick for her age as far as sports go.

"At our house during an Easter celebration, we had some friends over. One of the kids was much younger, and he would get very frustrated that he didn't win.

So they [Emma and the younger boy] had a race, and I saw her [Emma] purposefully slow down and let him pass and finish the race. He celebrated, and she celebrated with him.

"To me, that was an excellent example of her understanding that it didn't matter if she won. But she was going to help that other kid have that experience and have fun.

Knowing that he was probably going to be upset and mad if he lost, [she took] the time to think about someone else instead of always thinking about herself.

I was proud of her for doing it."

But how did he teach his young daughter empathy? What can you learn from his experience? The best way to tell what happened is to give his exact words:

"We really tried to instill a culture of sharing and helping others. I really think that with her, she was born an empathetic soul; we just decided to acknowledge it as often as we could so that she felt proud of her behavior.

"I will say that it is getting harder as she grows to find what line is appropriate. I often get questions from her when we see someone begging on the street and she asks 'Why don't we just share our money with them?'

"I try to give to people when I think it is safe [in order] to continue to foster her giving and empathetic nature, but I am also constantly worried that someone will end up taking advantage of her later in life if I don't teach her some of the harsher sides of life.

"I have to always remind myself of Mother Teresa and her quote, "Do it anyway," and remember that although there can be harm in being naive, there is good in being kind."

That's empathy.

3 Ways To Develop Empathy in Your Daughter

1. Point it out[6]

When your daughter is kind to others, praise her actions. In her article, The Caring Child: How to teach empathy, Mary Van Clay recommends telling children when you approve of what they do so they can begin to understand the difference between empathy and apathy.

For example, in the second case study, Sean let his daughter know how proud he was that she allowed her younger guest to win the race. What examples can you remember when your daughter showed empathy toward a sibling or another person? The next time you witness her being empathetic, mention it to her.

2. Model empathetic behavior at every opportunity[7]

In her article, Teaching Empathy: Evidence-based tips for fostering empathy in children, Gwen Dewar, PH.D. suggests parents demonstrate empathetic behavior for their children. For example, she recommends parents ask their children to imagine how other kids feel when they see people being victimized on television or in literature. In the first case study above, David discusses how he and his former wife provided examples of empathy for his daughters, Brooks and Blair to follow. What examples can you set for you daughter?

3. Help kids discover what they have in common with others[8]

Citing other research, Dr. Dewar suggests that kids feel empathy towards people with whom they share similarities or unpleasant experiences.

She wrote, "The more we can humanize the victims of distress or tragedy, the better kids will be able to respond with empathy."

For example, school children empathize with their peers from other states or countries. Sometimes their classes provide care packages to children who have been displaced by flooding like in Texas or earthquakes like in Tibet.

If empathy is a component of respecting others, then perhaps we need to show our girls how we respect others even when we don't agree or empathize with them.

Read the rest of my personal story, below, about the woman dropping off her son at school.

The woman in the car

Eventually, the woman drove around me like the other cars behind her. Everyone could see I was trying to park. But before that, I thought how my response would affect my daughter.

The entire incident lasted only a few seconds. But at that moment, instead of responding in anger, I put myself in that woman's position.

Was she already angry about something else that day? Was she late for work? You never know what someone else is going through at any given moment.

Why set a bad example for my daughter? Why make matters worse?

As the woman pulled her car up beside mine, she rolled down her window.

"Why didn't you drive away?" she demanded as she glared at me.

"Everyone can see I'm trying to park," I replied with a firm but calm voice. "Why didn't you go around?"

She paused, thought about it, and then drove away.

My six-year-old daughter who witnessed the whole thing could've seen my blow up at this woman and disrespect her over a misunderstanding that lasted 30 seconds.

Instead, she saw me have a tense but respectful verbal exchange with a fellow parent and driver one morning at school.

My daughter witnessed me maintaining respect for this other person and for myself—both at the same time.

Why didn't I say more?

Because I've learned my daughters copy my actions, I'm careful about how they see me treat people, particularly women. I could've scared my littlest one, ruined her day, or given her the false idea that women should be treated disrespectfully.

Some dads may think that I'm ridiculous or that I wimped out. But I'd ask those parents, "When is the last time you showed your daughters how you respect women, particularly women who are not relatives?

What kind of impression would you have made for your daughters if you were in my shoes?"

I'm not saying dads have to give in and allow people to walk all over us because that won't model self-respect. But we don't have to treat others like dirt either.

I realized long ago, by trial and error, when I'm out with my girls, my actions will be on their radar. My daughters will be watching what I do and repeat what I say.

And if your daughters are anything like mine, then your daughters will watch what you do and repeat what you say. How will you model respect for others—and for yourself—around your daughters?

What to do now?

Take another look at the six ways to teach your daughter about respect. Notice that these are techniques you'll have to practice with your daughter for them to stick. Think about which ones will work best with your parenting style.

Receive your free one-page guide of the six tricks to develop self-respect in your daughter without her knowing at: www.raisingyourdaughter.com/respect.

What's next

In this chapter, we discussed six techniques dads use to boost their daughters' self-respect and respect for other people. In the next chapter, we'll go a little deeper into why what you say to your daughter has an enormous bearing on her self-esteem.

You'll also discover what one father told his daughter years before her car accident ended up saving her life. Read the next chapter and find out.

CHAPTER 4

How to Get Your Daughter to Want to Listen to You Over and Over Again

Children always listen. They may not always do what you say, but they always listen, and they'll recall something you said years ago. ~ Mikal Nelson, author of The Quick Fix to Any Problem

Does it matter what you say to your daughter? More importantly, does it matter how you say it?

Imagine driving home one evening after a really long day. You'd just completed a 7-hour drive as the designated driver of a minibus full of kids on the high school track team.

You're finally heading home—envisioning yourself kicking back in your favorite recliner with your feet up, watching the game and drinking a brew, when— BAM!—without warning an oncoming car crosses into your lane and smashes into you head-on.

How would you react at that moment?

Liz, now 27, lived through it all just as an oncoming car careened in front of her as she drove home from work. According to Liz, her father's words saved her that night—something he had said years previously.

I want to share Liz's story. But first, I want to show you how you can talk to your daughter in a way that will encourage her to listen to you.

You'll discover how to listen to her better and spark conversations with her where she listens to you.

You'll also discover why the words you speak are so important to your daughter's future. Your words have a greater influence on her than you may realize.

7 Ways to Get Your Daughter to Listen to You Again

Here are seven ways to not only get your daughter to listen to what you say but also to help build her self-esteem. Read below and find out which ones you should start using today.

1. Ask about her day.

This is something I've had to remember to do over time. By sharing my experience with you now, I hope to help you make this simple tweak a lot sooner.

Of course, if you're like most dads, then you probably already know how important having regular conversation is to your daughter. People tend to confide in people they talk to the most.

By becoming one of those people your daughter confides in, you will be strengthening your father-daughter bond.

With my girls, I always ask each of them to tell me about her day. My daughter, Daniella, always tells me about her math teacher, Mr. Gallagher, and how he stares at the students like a zombie.

Sometimes she tells me about pranks she plays with her friends or how they become excited when she shows them her latest drawings of anime characters.

My daughter, Mikayla, tells me about the word she learned in kindergarten that day or about the finger painting she made at the art table.

When I ask them about their days, my girls know 1) I'm interested, 2) I'm going to listen, and 3) I'm actually going to engage them in conversation. I'll use verbal cues like, "Hmm" or "Okay" or whatever is appropriate. Sometimes I'm going to laugh at their stories.

Other times, they're going to ask me a question, and then I'm going to answer. I give them eye contact. Sometimes I might be busy preparing my world-famous spaghetti, working out in the garage, playing video games or burying my nose in the computer screen or smartphone.

But I make myself available to them. The point is— we talk.

Now, what if you're thinking: "I'm not a talker, so how is this supposed to work for me?"

If that's the case, then I'd encourage you to be a good listener first. Ask your daughter about her day and listen to her response.

Do something that indicates to her that you're interested in what she has to say. Look at her even if she's looking away.

Avoid forcing her to talk. Instead, allow this technique to work for you over time as you both gradually become more comfortable with it.

Also, try to remember the names of friends, teachers and other people she mentions because it shows you've been listening to her all along.

Remember: Don't interrogate; just communicate.

2. Spend more time listening to her.

We sometimes focus so much energy on communicating our desires and demands that we forget to take time out to listen to our daughters.

When I served in the Army, I supervised several subordinate soldiers. Whenever they failed to complete a task, I immediately tore into them and I didn't care what they had to say. I thought their reasons were just whiny excuses.

Then one day I asked a rhetorical question, "Why can't you guys do anything right?" I didn't expect an answer, but I got an earful.

They told me how they were being pulled in different directions, asked to do things they didn't know how to do, and so on. Using my own words, I then repeated back to them what they had just said to me.

So what do you think happened next?

Together we fixed the problems, built up morale and made the team function better. This all happened as a result of my listening to my team and then responding to their needs by working together with them. But something else happened, too. I tell you more in a moment.

In the same way, I began listening to my girls.

In both cases, my soldiers and my daughters did something unexpected. They both opened up and began communicating with me more frequently. As it turns out, listening to them built trust and allowed me to empathize with them.

Can you see how listening to your daughter will not only get her to listen to you but also knock down the invisible wall you may have between you and get her to open up to you more often? If you want to be heard, first you must listen.

3. Tell her little truths about herself.

Do you know the secret to having a good day?

I often ask my daughter Kayla this question whenever she feels sad. I know that things in life happen and there are times when the only response to a situation is to be sad or angry with the world. But more often than not, we have the ability to choose.

Instead of just telling your daughter about Santa Claus or tales of the Easter Bunny, tell her the truth about what you believe about her.

"You can choose to be happy."

"I believe you'll have a great day today."

"You can do it."

"You got this."

Get her to believe in herself by telling her what you think about her.

Whatever words you pour into your daughter's mind, make sure those words are real and inspiring because she'll draw on those words long after she's grown up and left home to pursue her dreams.

4. Turn your criticisms to compliments.

When I was a kid, I hated getting criticized. I still hate it. The reason I hate it is because I rarely get any constructive criticism or compliments about what I'm doing right. Can you relate to that?

Now, put yourself in your daughter's shoes. Ask yourself, "How are my words critical of her? How can I find ways to compliment her on the things she's doing well?"

As fathers, we need to recognize that screwing up is a way of life for some of our children. But to always point out their flaws and failures only convinces our daughters that they are failures.

Of course, great dads like you already know this is not how we want our daughters to think of themselves.

That's why it's important to compliment her when she cleans her room or puts away her things without being told. It's important to recognize her when she empties the washing machine, helps set the table, or completes her homework.

No matter how small or how big her results, compliment what she's doing right and help her correct what she's doing wrong, constructively.

For example, you could say something like this:

"I love you ..., and next time will you be careful to ..."

"I know you were trying to help when you ..., but it would be more helpful to ..."

"It's great to ... but a better time to do that is when ... Do you see why?"

Use these examples as a guide. Think about how you might start a conversation with your daughter using your own words. Ask yourself: How would I say that?

5. Keep it brief.

Don't ramble on. I still struggle with this one. It's tough, I know. But after you start to see your daughter's eyes glaze over because of your long-winded speeches, you'll realize that she no longer understands the words that are coming out of your mouth. To get your daughter to listen to you, keep your speeches brief.

Otherwise, she'll just wait until you've finished speaking and give you the required response, "Yes, daddy," without having heard the point of your lecture.

6. Give advance notice.

This works well with younger girls, but frankly, it's good to use at any age. The reason I say this is because, in my house, bedtime for my 6-year-old is like preparing people for a fire drill. You'd better give advanced warning or they'll freak out.

So by letting you girls know in advance that it's almost bedtime (or it's almost time to leave the house, so go use the toilet now) helps soften any blowback.

It also reduces your stress level because her overreaction is less likely to annoy you the first time you tell her to do something.

Even if you have to repeat yourself, at least she's received fair warning and will more likely comply without any drama. Just know that you may have to repeat yourself—which brings me to my next tip.

7. Repeat yourself.

Is talking to your daughter like talking to a brick wall? Sometimes my girls stare at me like I'm speaking Martian, and I don't know if what I'm saying is getting through. Does this happen to you?

You may find it helpful to repeat yourself. I don't just mean repeatedly tell them to brush their teeth or go to bed or pick up their clothes. I'm referring to life-lessons you want your daughters to learn.

Sometimes, you'll find it necessary to repeatedly tell your daughters, "Try again if at first you don't succeed." You should frequently tell them to stay away from people who get you into trouble.

Or, in Liz's case, repeatedly tell her how to handle her car in the event of an accident.

Below, read Liz's story about what her father repeatedly taught her about driving. As you read further, think about what life-lessons you want to instill in your daughter.

Liz's Story

The best way to tell what happened to Liz is to give her exact words:

"My dad's words literally saved my life that night.

"I was driving home around 10:00 one night on a dark, winding road. As I drove around a bend, I saw a car coming straight towards me. I didn't have time to react or honk my horn. But my dad's words echoed clearly in my head, 'Don't jerk the steering wheel. Drift to the shoulder.'

"Everything happened within seconds, but it seemed like an eternity. With my dad's instructions guiding me, I narrowly avoided being hit head on. Instead, the other driver clipped the side of the car and sent me spinning out into the middle of the road several times.

"From the time I was young, I remember my dad always mentioned what we (my brothers and I) should do if we ever got into a car accident. I also remembered my dad's words to help me relax.

He repeatedly told us that if a car was coming at us head-on, 'don't jerk your steering wheel. Otherwise, the car will end up flipped upside down in a ditch while the other car drives away without a scratch.'

"It's the craziest thing, but I just sat back in my seat and went with the momentum of the car. I didn't even get the chance to freak out until my car stopped. I saw headlights coming at me, but only the entire driver's side of my car got crushed in.

"Later as the cops came to inspect the accident, a policeman said to me, 'Ma'am, we can see exactly what happened from the tire tracks on the road. I just want to let you know that you handled that car perfectly.'

"Another officer came to me later and shared, 'I see a lot of car accidents every day, but this one was just beautiful.'

"I never thought I'd ever hear a cop describe an accident as 'beautiful.' They almost seemed shocked that I'd come out without a scratch. I told them that it was thanks to my dad's teaching—words he'd spoken years ago.

"It's crazy what you actually remember in a moment of crisis, right?"

Why Liz's story should matter to you and your daughter?

Liz's story is unique, I know. After all, how many times have you heard someone's daughter avoiding a car accident like that?

But what isn't unique is that dad's all over the world are teaching their daughters all kinds of life lessons like this just by speaking to them and sharing their knowledge just like Liz's dad.

If you're anything like him, then you'll probably understand how important it is to share your knowledge with your daughter.

You may also know how important it is to use your words to build up her up instead of tearing her down and to give her the knowledge she'll need to handle herself in the future.

What you say today has the power to change your daughter's life tomorrow.

What to do?

Take a moment to think about how you speak to your daughter. Do you speak in a manner that connects with her? Do your words build her up or tear her down?

Review the advice in this chapter to help you talk to you daughter in a way that connects the two of you together. Give it time. The point is to use these techniques daily without giving up if you don't see immediate progress.

Soon you'll discover which ones work best for you and your daughter, and you'll come rely on them over and over. I encourage you to start today because these techniques take time to build upon. Remember to:

1) Spend time listening.

2) Give you daughter positive reinforcement.

3) Turn criticisms to compliments.

4) Keep your long-winded "speeches" brief.

5) Give advance notice.

6) Repeat.

7) On the next page, read more about Liz and her father to find out more tips to help you boost your daughter's self-esteem.

8) You can download your free one-page copy of these seven ways to convince your daughter to listen at: http://www.raisingyourdaughter.com/listen.

Up Next

Now that you've had a chance to look at how to speak to your daughter in a way that connects with her, in the next chapter I want to reveal ways to help you boost her self-image.

I'll also share stories of several people who'll help you understand why your presence in your daughter's life matters.

But first, read an excerpt of my interview with Liz. From her story, find out how your words and actions could shape your daughter's future.

A Daughter's Advice

Here is an excerpt of my interview with Liz Tate, author of Awaken: Eliminate Your Ruts, Pursue Your Dreams, And Live Life To Its Fullest.

So tell me about your dad.

My dad wasn't perfect at all. There were many things he learned through trial and error. But, he's been such a huge impact on my upbringing. And the biggest thing I can say is that he has been a huge part of my life.

Of all the stories I can think of, it all boils down to this. Not only did he say he loved me, but he also showed me he loved me by playing with me and being a part of my life.

That's pretty awesome.

What advice can you give dads who desperately want to know how they should be raising their daughters?

Well, I have to say the biggest thing is spending time with your daughter. It doesn't have to cost a lot of money. It doesn't have to be fancy.

But take the time to get to know her.

That means, from the time she's a toddler all the way through adulthood. If you start that foundation young, then that relationship is going to work out as she gets older.

Also, boost your daughter's self-esteem. I can't tell you how important this is. It doesn't matter if she's 3 or 30. Your daughter needs to hear from her dad that she is more important than anyone else. You know? It's not just the words, though.

You can tell her you love her. You can tell her she's important and that she matters and that she'll make a difference in the world.

But the words won't be enough. Because if you tell your daughter you love her, but don't show her then it's just empty rhetoric. It's not going to make a difference in her life.

But if you tell her and show her by actually being active involved in her life and spending time with her, then that's going to make such a huge difference.

My dad didn't have much money. He struggled to provide for a family of seven. He didn't have a lot of money to give, but his active involvement in my life has been the greatest gift that I could have.

I'm now 27, and he's still my go-to person when I'm in trouble. He's the person I want advice from because he's been there through so many difficult times when I needed help.

My mom had a dad who never once told her that he loved her until he was on his deathbed when she was 60 years old. So she lived 60 years before hearing her dad say, "I love you."

That had a big impact on her life. I know when she was looking for a husband, she wanted one who was going to be a great father to her kids. She found our father. He is a great dad.

It's great to get a woman's point of view about these things because frankly, guys don't often sit around discussing their daughters often.

I was so excited when I heard about your book because I think it's such a huge thing.

In college, when I saw a girl throwing herself at a guy or being in a string of relationships, she either had a father who was not in her life at all or who was emotionally distant.

I could just look at her and say, "You don't have a good relationship with your father, do you?" She would say, "No, I don't" or "He's not in my life at all."

It hit me then, "Wow. I have a great dad that God's given me because he's been there."

I did remember one more thing that I wanted to say. Teach your daughters some useful skills, like how to put oil in her car or how to paint a house or whatever it is. Teach useful skills like my dad did, and I appreciate that now, today.

What fathers don't know could hurt their daughters. Turn the page to find out more.

CHAPTER 5

Why Your Presence Matters in Your Daughter's Life More Than You Know

It's easier to build up a child than to repair an adult. - Unknown

In this chapter, you'll discover what you need to know about your daughter's self-image.

I'll also reveal warning signs that may suggest your daughter has a low self-image and recommend ways you can help your daughter overcome her insecurities and achieve her goals in life.

But first, I want to share the stories of five people to show you just how much influence you have over your daughter.

As you read about the lives of these people, think about what ideas you can take away from them and apply to your parenting style.

Chelsea's story

Even when a father abandons his daughter emotionally, the father-figure is so important to a daughter that she'll find one elsewhere (and you'd better hope it's a good one).

Chelsea, a 21-year-old college student in West Virginia, never had a close relationship with her dad. Though he remained a part of her life, she felt he'd never really cared what she was doing or where she was going.

He seemed to care instead only about himself. At times, she felt like she grew up without a father at all.

Fortunately, Chelsea's grandfather Freddy, now 86, stepped in and took care of her. This quiet and shy Korean War veteran was the only man who gave her the fatherly love and support she needed as a child. In his own way, he guided her when her father didn't.

"It's kind of weird," she explained. "It's not like the deepest thing that anybody could ever say to a kid," she said, referring to her grandfather. "But every time I'd see him when I was little, he would give me $5, and I thought that was the coolest thing ever. That was a lot of money when you were six."

Simple acts like these made a difference in Chelsea's life.

Now, think about your daughter for a moment. How do you express your love and support for her? How will she remember your presence in her life? Moments like these shape our daughters' futures. Moments like these describe who we are as dads.

Chelsea believes her grandfather can best be described by this simple word: generous.

"That's how I've tried to be throughout my life," she said. "I would have never learned that if it weren't for my grandpa because my dad didn't teach me. My grandfather's so amazing. I'll always be thinking about how to help other people because that's how he raised me."

Because of her struggles with low self-esteem, Chelsea wrote a book to help young women carrying the same heavy burden of self-doubt and loathing she did as a teen. In Imperfectly Perfect: How to Get up from Rock Bottom, Create Habits to Love Yourself, and Learn to Maintain a Growth Mindset, Chelsea shares her story of how she overcame her feelings of failure. Plus, she reveals what young girls should do now to improve their self-image.

Next, find out what our next father does when he plans his playtime with his two little princesses. Is it something you can do in your home? Read below and find out.

Omer's story

"Kids spell love, T-I-M-E," explained Omer, father of two girls, ages 4 and 2, and a boy, aged 6 months. He is also the author of the book, Give and Grow Rich: Change Your Mind, Change Your Money.

"If you don't make T-I-M-E for them, then that's telling them, 'I don't love you; I don't have enough time for you.'"

When he's playing with his kids, Omer is the type of father who not only turns off his smartphone and shuts down his computer but also gets down on the floor and romps around with his toddlers.

"Kids love when you get down on your knees or squat down and talk to them at eye level, and laugh with them and act silly with them, dance and act crazy," he shared.

Omer believes, since his kids love to frolic and play games with their dad, they will want to continue to experience fun times with him well into their teenage years.

He believes fathers should take an active interest in the things their kids like to do in order to strengthen the bond between parent and child.

"If you take an interest in the TV shows they're interested in or the pop bands they're interested in or use the social media they use, then you're learning from them.

"I guess if I could sum it up: kids aren't a nuisance. Kids are to be enjoyed. So enjoy them. Learn from them. And make time for them. By doing all those things, you'll love them even more."

Omer has an excellent relationship with his son and daughters. Unfortunately, not every daughter grows up with the benefit of having a great father.

What can you learn from Omer and apply to your relationship with your little girl? Think about that as you read the next story about a girl who had a very different experience.

Julie's story

For Julie, alcoholism struck her childhood like a twister, leaving behind a poor little girl, broken, abandoned, and abused.

As teenagers, Julie's parents had gotten married and later, had three children. Julie, whose name I've changed to protect her privacy, was the only girl.

As children, she and her brothers always played together outside their home in Sydney, Australia. Every day revealed new wonder and excitement for her until, at age 6, Julie saw her drunken dad pound his fist into her mother's face over and over until she fell to the floor.

That was the end of her childhood. Things got worse over the years as her father drank heavily. By the time she was 9, Julie's parents were divorced and her father moved away. Because of a hip injury, though, he couldn't find work, so he drank even more.

Though he never abused her or her brothers, Julie's father was still the same monster he had been before he left.

Whenever he'd come to visit, the violence continued—a slap to the head, a push to the floor, a yank of the hair, or worse.

By then, she'd lost all respect for him. But her anger towards him intensified after her uncle sexually abused her. Because she believed his alcoholism clouded his ability to realize what she was going through, Julie kept silent.

Years later, Julie finally revealed the truth but the damage had already been done. She hated her father. He hadn't wanted to be a part of her life. He'd missed her graduation. She'd only see him occasionally.

Now, 30 years later, Julie is slowly picking up the shattered pieces of her life. She visits her father rarely.

She feels the way he chose to deal with his problems robbed her of her childhood. Julie also believes her sense of confidence and security has been lost.

She doesn't trust people because she believes the one person who was supposed to protect her—her father— was never there. She doesn't know what a healthy father-daughter relationship looks like.

Today Julie's still searching for the lost pieces of her childhood. Of course, Julie's story is an extreme case of parental absenteeism.

However, if you're like most dads, then you probably know that abandoning, abusing, or emotionally distancing yourself from a child for whatever reason can have an enormous impact on her future.

To a lesser extent, consider the effects of divorce, marital separation, incarceration, military deployment, long hours at work, or any other form of separation can have on a child. What can you do to spend more time with your daughter?

In the next story, you'll meet Sean, father of two girls. What's he doing to ensure he spends more time with his younger daughter? Read below to find out. See whether you can do something similar for your daughter.

Sean's story

Sean, a physical therapist in California and author of Super Spine Neck Check: Chronic Neck Pain Relief Once and For All, is able to arrange his busy schedule to fit in weekly playtime with his daughters, Emma, age 7, and Alexis, age 3.

Sean takes Monday's off and works from home to spend time with his littlest lady. One thing he's learned as a father of two daughters is that he's got to be willing to leave his comfort zone and hang with the girls on their level.

"You've got to take the time to enjoy what she likes, which may not be what you like," he admitted. "I'm home with my younger daughter Alexis, and I actually sit down and make sure we play dolls for half an hour."

Before they begin, Sean sets his timer on his smartphone for 30 minutes and plays with his daughter until the timer goes off. He dedicates that time just for the two of them so they can play with whatever she wants.

Then, it's back to work. But before times up, it's lady's choice, and his little princess usually chooses to play with Barbie. Sean says he feels silly, but it's something his daughter loves doing.

"I dedicate that time to just me and her, and we play dolls. It's not something that I would necessarily like to do, but it's something that she likes to do. I try and make sure I've blocked out and actually dedicated the time where I'm focused on her."

Like many fathers, Sean is doing all he can to spend more time at home. But no matter how much time we spend with our daughters, as they get older, people will say harsh things about her for their own selfish reasons.

So what should you say to fix it when it happens? In the next story, find out what one father said to his daughter after a comment about her went viral.

Gabby's story

If you're like most men, then you'd probably agree that no girl should be objectified or targeted by sexual deviants on social media.

Yet many girls deal with that kind of behavior all the time. Imagine your daughter having to deal with this one day, too.

What would you tell her?

87

How would you react?

Here's what happened to the daughter of former Boston Red Sox pitcher, Curt Schilling:

Two men posted sexually explicit comments about her on Twitter.

In an article for the goodmenproject.com, Mike Kasdan reported how one tweet became a nightmare for Gabby Schilling and her father because of a couple of Twitter trolls.

Earlier in 2015, Salve Regina University accepted Gabby as a student where she'd pitch for the school's softball team. Her father, Curt, a former pitcher himself, proudly sent a tweet about his daughter's great news along with her picture.

Unfortunately, several men replied to Schilling's tweet with insanely vulgar and inappropriate comments about what sexual acts they'd like to perform on Gabby.

Eventually, Curt tracked two of them down, identified the men by name on his blog and posted a response in defense of his daughter. The men subsequently lost their jobs.

On his blog, Schilling wrote to his daughter6, "Gabby, I know you're likely embarrassed and for that I apologize. But as we have talked about, there is no situation ever in your life, where it's ok for any 'man' to talk about you, or any other woman this way."

Schilling continued by saying, "Like any dad reading this the only thing I need you to leave this home with when you head to college is the knowledge that I love you more than life itself, and there is NOTHING I would not do to protect you. And while it may sound corny, it's nothing I'd ever be shy about saying in public, ever."

To learn more about this story and Curt Schilling's response, visit goodmenproject.com.

What you should know about her self-image

The important thing to know about self-image is this: it starts with a choice—her choice. Teach your daughter to appreciate who she is, no matter what people may think of her.

In early 2015, Unilever, maker of Dove soap, created a beauty campaign to see how women viewed themselves. The video they produced showed real women making real choices about their own self-image. Watch the video and picture your daughter making this same choice every day. The results may surprise you. You can look at the video online at youtube.com.

Do you think your daughter should have a favorable opinion of herself regardless of what images she may see online, in movies, on television or on a sign? The question is: How do you accomplish this? How do you strengthen her self-image every day?

Imagine that her self-image is like the foundation of a building. Every day, another brick gets added to the life she's building. Your job is to pour your words and actions into her life to strengthen her foundation.

Eventually, she will be able to support any pressure placed on her, but you have to keep building her up every day. Tell your daughter what you believe about her to be true.

"You're smart."

"I enjoy spending time with you."

"I believe in you."

Whatever you say to boost your daughter's self-image, make sure you add it to her foundation. She will need those words to maintain a positive image of herself or, at the very least, to make it harder for someone else to tear her down.

Make her resilient to the contrary opinions and criticisms she'll face in life.

Also, make sure you back up your words with action. If you tell her she's smart, treat her like she's smart.

If you say you enjoy her company, then act like you enjoy her company. If you say you believe in her, show her you believe in her.

In other words, to boost your daughter's self-image, demonstrate to her what you think to be true about her.

In his spoken word performance, To the Boys Who May One Day Date My Daughter, Jesse Parent expresses his devotion to his daughter while warning potential suitors not to break her heart.

He weaves tender soliloquies of love for his young princess with passionate declarations of vengeance against any man who attempts to harm her.

Yet his entertaining delivery captures the emotions of so many fathers.

You can see his performance on youtube.com.

Remember, when building your daughter's self-image, back up your words and action.

So, now that you know why a positive self-image is important, how will you know when your daughter's self-image is low? Below you'll find a few warnings signs which may help you find the answer.

5 Warning Signs Your Daughter Has a Low Self-Image (and what you can do about it)[9]

If you're like most dads, then you probably know your daughter better than most people on the planet, right? If your daughter has a low self-image, then you may recognize one or two behaviors on this list.

Even if your daughter commits none of these acts now, take a look at them and see which ones could apply to her in the future.

1) She is unable to leave the house without make-up.

Your daughter needs make-up to go anywhere or she wears too much.

Tip: Let her know how attractive she looks without make-up. She needs to hear that from her dad, and she needs to hear that often enough for that message to sink in.

2) She can't handle genuine praise.

Your daughter cringes when she receives a compliment. Accepting a compliment is never easy when you're not used to receiving them.

Tip: Compliment her more often and not just on her appearance. Praise her efforts. For example, tell her why you admire the way she cleaned her room, practiced her flute, or helped prepare dinner.

3) She compares herself to attractive women in the media.

Your daughter compares herself to images of beautiful women she sees in movies, on television, online, and on social media.

Tip: Teach your daughter that media images give a false representation of real women and are meant only to sell products and services.

You can even find pictures of famous actresses and singers before they've been made-up for the camera; images where these celebrities look like regular people.

Show these images to your daughter, so she can better understand the false representation behind the advertising-style images.

4) She is overly critical of her appearance.

Your daughter criticizes her appearance often and doesn't always like how she looks.

Tip: For every self-criticism she gives, require her to say something positive about her appearance. Encourage her to focus on her features that make her unique.

5) She feels her body is too fat or too thin.

Your daughter feels she is either too thick or too thin. Often girls are bullied because of their weight or see themselves as too fat or too thin when everyone else can plainly see she is neither.

Tip: Talk to her and find out what's going on. Give her time to confide in you. If she refuses to tell you, then don't give up after one attempt.

At some point, girls who exhibit these warning signs may need help beyond what most parents can provide. Eating disorders, body dysmorphic disorders, and other body image disorders are best treated by a medical professional.

If your daughter's condition has progressed beyond your level of expertise, then stop waiting and get help.

What to do now?

1) Let your daughter know she is loved for who she is, not for how she looks.

2) As a father, you don't have to be perfect; you just have to be present.

3) Review the 5 warning signs that your daughter may have a low self-image.

4) Read my interview with Sean who shares his tips and experience to add to your parenting tool belt.

5) Get your cheat sheet of the five warning signs your daughter has low self-esteem and what to do about it at: www.raisingyourdaughter.com/signs.

What's next?

In this chapter, you discovered how other dads spend time with their daughters. You've also learned about the importance your presence has in your daughter's life.

Then we covered things to know about self-image and discussed warning signs, which may reveal your daughter has a low self-image.

In chapter six, we'll talk about perseverance and how to teach your daughter to achieve success despite difficulties she may face.

But first, find out more about Sean's success at being the best dad ever to his two little girls. Turn the page and discover his simple little secret.

Fatherly Advice

Sean is a busy physical therapist from California with two young daughters. He and his wife struggled to find balance until finally things fell into place.

Read my interview with Sean Sumner, author of Neck Check: Chronic Neck Pain Relief Once and For All.

How did you react when you had your first daughter?

We found out early on. We didn't wait. I was a little shocked. I come from a family of all boys. I have several brothers and no sisters. But I was so happy because I knew my wife really wanted a little girl. But I also had a feeling of, "I have absolutely no idea what to do or how to act around girls or how to raise girls or anything like that."

How did you adjust?

Everything that we did was by trial and error. Even my mom, who watches the kids now and then, never had to raise any girls in her life. It was always boys. We didn't even have nieces in the family to help us adjust. It was definitely by trial and error trying to figure out what worked. Sometimes, I asked friends who I thought were doing really well. Overall, we just experienced it and tried what worked.

What are you doing right now that seems to be working for you?

Well, I would say that one of the things that I do with my girls is I allow them some of my time where they can be in charge of me, and they can have the responsibility. Usually during play time, they tell me, "Okay, we need to do this." And they have a little bit of authority over me for a short time. And I've found that to be very helpful because, instead of me always being the one in charge, giving them that small little bit where they can be in charge helps them. It works really well for their self-esteem.

I incorporate that with both my girls—my older girl not as much anymore, but definitely my younger one. We take the time to play, and during that play, if she wants to be the one in charge, I definitely let her have the opportunity.

That's good. That helps their self-esteem, boosts their confidence and helps them with their decision-making ability as well.

Yeah, I think definitely it helps. I find they tend to make better decisions afterwards.

If they're in charge for a small time, they'll actually go through the same scenarios that we go through on a daily basis.

They'll say, "Okay it's time for bed," or, "It's time to eat." Then, I'll act out a little bit like they might. Or I'll act out in different ways and see how they respond.

Typically they'll respond really well and say, "No, you need to eat your vegetables," or "No, it's time for bed."

I've found that allowing them to come to those conclusions on their own helps later on when I'm really trying to get them to go to sleep or eat their vegetables.

Many dads are now facing the same challenges you once faced. What other advice can you share with them?

Well, the first comment I usually make to guys is, "Welcome to the world of pink and fluffy," because it doesn't matter if you choose to do pink and girly stuff. You can't avoid it because everyone around you is going to give you flack.

Just welcome it, embrace it, and get over yourself and get into it. That's usually my first piece of advice.

Secondly, you've got to take the time to enjoy what she likes, which may not be what you like. When I take a day off and work from home, I'm home with my younger daughter.

I actually sit down and make sure we play dolls for half an hour. I set a timer on my phone so, when the timer goes off, it sounds like my phone is ringing.

Then I tell her I have a phone call, and I gotta start work. But I dedicate that time to just play dolls with her. It feels very silly.

It's not something that I would necessarily like to do, but it's something that she likes to do. I make sure I block off the time and dedicate it to focus on her.

The third thing is you want to make sure that you incorporate her in the things that you like. My older daughter is old enough to help with chores and home improvement things.

So when I go out and I'm using a drill gun or a screw gun, I make sure that she comes out there, too. As soon as she was old enough to hold a screw gun, she started using it.

When I changed a tire, I had her come over to the car and do whatever she could, and it worked to her advantage because she gained confidence. Even though it took a small chunk of my time, it made our relationship much, much better. Make sure you give her time to do some of the stuff that you like or you feel is important as well.

What you should know about your daughter and perseverance. Turn the page to find out.

CHAPTER 6

How to Convince Your Daughter to Persevere Even When She Wants to Quit

Perseverance is the great divide between failure and success; between defeat and victory.

Some guys might think this chapter can be summed up in one simple sentence: Don't let your daughter quit. And you know what? They'd de absolutely wrong because before I learned this one thing, I used to think that way too.

At times, I felt like I was better at sprouting gray hair from my scalp than motivating my daughter. Eventually, I figured out this one thing that helped her go further than any words could have done alone.

That one thing was this: Don't simply tell your daughter to keep going; show her how.

Now if you're anything like most dads I've interviewed, then you already know that teaching your daughter perseverance involves showing her how it's done. Because like it or not, there will be days when she'll want to quit and her self-esteem will plummet unless she knows what to do.

What can you do now to help your daughter before that happens?

Let's discuss several things you can do to teach your daughter perseverance, so she'll be able to face her challenges and be successful in the future. But before we dive in, let's talk about what you should know about perseverance.

What to Say To Her about perseverance

Like most people, I'm sure you recall that Thomas Edison invented the light bulb. That's not big news. In fact, it's something we all take for granted.

But what must people don't realize is that Edison made 1,000 unsuccessful attempts to create the light bulb before he finally got it right. Thankfully, he persevered.

Fortunately, most people won't have to try that hard to accomplish a goal. Still you may want to help your daughter understand that even famous people must overcome challenges more often than we realize.

For example:

J.K. Rowling, author of the Harry Potter series, has sold over 450 million books, has 4.6 million Twitter followers, and amassed a fortune—yet her original manuscript was rejected by 12 different publishers.

Dr. Seuss, aka Theodor Seuss Geisel, whose books have become a standard by which all children's literature is judged, was rejected 27 times before finally getting his first book published.

The Climax-Fisher Knights High School girls' basketball team, a relatively unknown group of girls from Minnesota, appeared on the local news when they snapped an 84-game losing streak to win a game everyone, including their coach, thought they'd lose.

And then, there's Brooks ...

When the going gets tough ...

When faced with the difficult decision to either quit her club volleyball team or finish out the season, 14-year-old Brooks found herself immersed in controversy.

For reasons unknown, she found herself on the outside of the team looking in. Winning is difficult enough when everyone on the team likes one another, but imagine trying to win with people you hate.

Of course, hate may be too strong a word to describe the feelings between Brooks and some of her teammates. Still, she played under stressful conditions as a member of that team.

Her father David credits her with being able to put aside her feelings and work with her teammates to win.

Naturally, as parents, we sense when something's wrong in our children's' lives, and we want to put a stop to it. We want them to keeping going, pushing them to greater success—urging them to try harder.

However, at some point, we may need to ask ourselves these questions:

Am I pushing too hard?

Am I asking her to do better than her best?

Shouldn't I recognize when my daughter just isn't having fun anymore?

Am I forcing her to participate?

Is my relationship with my daughter worth sacrificing for this?

I always try to remember that perseverance does not mean push to adherence. That may sound silly to some people, but what I mean is this: If I didn't force my daughter to stick around, would she still be here?

When things got worse for Brooks, her father David gave her his blessing to leave the team. But she replied, "No, Dad. I'm sticking to it. I made a commitment to my teammates. I want to stick this out to the end of the season."

One thing to understand is that David didn't force his daughter to stay on the team. She chose to stay. She decided to persevere. Despite her situation, Brooks chose to tough it out and continue to participate.

But, why?

At the heart of her desire to continue playing for the team rested the opportunity for her to decide for herself.

Remember that when someone decides to keep going, it's by choice.

To successfully encourage your daughter to persevere, you'll need to give her a choice as well, just like David gave his daughter Brooks.

In addition to perseverance, David admits he's tried to teach Brooks how to relate to others as well.

"Even though they're teammates and you don't like them, you still have to play with them, if you're going to be successful," he said. "That's one of those life lessons that … it's a hard one to learn."

Why should you teach your daughter about perseverance and what does it have to do with her self-esteem? The answer is everything.

When she believes she can achieve something no matter what happens, she'll have the confidence to handle almost any situation.

Without that ability, she'll never move forward. She'll quit every time life gets too hard.

What can you do to teach your daughter to persevere when times get tough?

6 Simple Ways to Help Your Daughter Persevere Even If She Wants To Quit

Here are some principles you'll want to instill in your daughter to help her persevere when she feels like quitting.

1. Set realistic goals.

Help her set realistic goals that she will be able to achieve. Use the 5-step S.M.A.R.T. method to help you. First, work with her to set a specific goal.

What exactly does she want to accomplish? My daughter wants to learn to play the flute better by practicing more often this year.

Then, help her to make her goal measurable. Figure out together how long she will take or how many repetitions she will complete. For example, my daughter decided to practice at least 30 minutes per day, five days per week.

Next, work together to craft an achievable goal. Use action-oriented words like, "I am going to." For instance, my daughter says, 'I'm going to practice my flute five days per week before I watch television or play on the computer."

Furthermore, guide her so that her goal is realistic. My daughter doesn't expect to play at Carnegie Hall or headline the middle school symphony orchestra. However, she's set a goal to learn one or two new songs per month.

Finally, the goal must have a timeframe, so help her determine a realistic timeframe. How long will the goal take to accomplish? For example, my daughter wants to improve her skills by the end of the school year.

As you implement these steps to develop goals with your daughter, remember to make the goals enjoyable. Also, together you should review her progress regularly and hold her accountable for sticking to the plan.

2. Believe in her. [10]

This one seems obvious. While telling your daughter how much you believe in her certainly helps, showing her works even better.

How do you do that?

Instead of pushing her into something you want her to do, encourage her to pursue her own interests.

Then help her follow through. For example, if she wants to be a veterinarian, take her to a petting zoo. Study animals with her online. If she wants to learn to cook, teach her how to make scrambled eggs or French toast.

Don't just tell her she can do something; find ways for her to explore, experiment with, and start practicing.

3. Teach her to believe in herself.

Do you remember the children's book, The Little Engine That Could by Watty Piper? It's an old story about a little train engine that wasn't afraid to try to climb up tracks around a mountain. When faced with doubt, it repeated to itself, "I think I can. I think I can."

Consider how many people ignore those simple little words in their own lives. Those words can make a difference in the way your daughter feels about herself.

Think of it this way. You wouldn't want her to develop a negative self-image by believing something like, "I can't do this. I'll never get it right." Instead, you'd want her to believe in herself by saying, "I can do this. I'm going to get better."

Teach your daughter to use positive statements like these to motivate herself to continue her climb like that little engine.

4. Practice, practice, practice.

My friend, M.D. Stokes, once told me his secret to success as a musician. He practiced piano for years, teaching himself to play by ear.

As a young man, he honed his craft in bars and nightclubs before moving on to play exclusively in churches on Sunday mornings.

Eventually, he became a gospel recording artist, released a CD, and traveled all over the world with his group.

One day he shared his secret with me that I've never forgotten.

He explained that practice doesn't make perfect. Perfection is unattainable. Instead, think of practice this way: Practice makes permanent.

When you practice something long enough, it will become second nature. As a result, you'll build your confidence because you'll know you can accomplish whatever you set out to do.

Practice is the key to becoming not only more competent but also becoming more confident.

Build your daughter's confidence by encouraging her to practice whatever skill she wants to improve.

5. Celebrate her victories (even if they're small).

Whenever your daughter does something positive or puts forth a real effort to accomplish her goals, reinforce that behavior by acknowledging her work.

Encourage her at every milestone. Celebrate her successes every step of the way.

For example, I know my daughter is working on being more responsible, so when she cleans her room without being asked, I applaud her effort and watch her face light up.

Avoid, however, giving gifts as a way of acknowledging her successes.

Why?

The reason is that when you always give a gift (even for the smallest things) your daughter will expect to receive one every time.

And, at some point when she doesn't receive a gift, she'll believe that it's because she's done something wrong. Therefore, encourage her with verbal praise instead.

Nevertheless, don't wait until your daughter makes the honor roll or wins a seat on student council before you acknowledge her triumph.

Acknowledge her success whenever and wherever you see it. She won't always win, but at least she'll continue to try if she knows she has your support.

6. Motivate her to keep going.

Naturally, dads want to encourage their daughters to never give up—don't quit. I say those words, too. But, then I thought, I always say that—don't do this or you better not do that. So instead of telling my daughter what she couldn't do, I decided to tell her what she could do. You know—frame it in the positive:

You can do it, sweetie. I believe in you. You got this.

What about you and your daughter? Are your words inspiring her to continue? Take a moment to consider how your words encourage her to move forward.

If she's old enough, you may want to ask if your words help her. If they do, then keep using them.

If not, then ask her how you can do better. It's humbling. I know. But you may discover something that could make a difference in her life.

What to do?

1) Help her set goals for herself.

2) Believe in her and teach her to believe in herself.

3) Build her confidence by encouraging her to practice in whatever area she needs to improve.

4) Celebrate her victories with her no matter how small.

5) Motivate her with words that build her up.

6) Download your free one-page guide of these six ways to help your daughter persevere at: www.raisingyourdaughter.com/persevere.

What's next

We've covered what you and your daughter should know about perseverance.

We've also talked about well-known figures and ordinary people who have shown grit in their lives.

Finally, we've looked at six principles to help you to teach your daughter perseverance.

Next, we'll discuss boosting her confidence one step further. Unfortunately, she won't always be able to deal with life on her terms.

What happens when she encounters roadblocks and setbacks that are beyond her control?

How do you teach her to overcome adversity? You'll discover ways to do that in the following chapter.

CHAPTER 7

Secrets to Helping Her Overcome Adversity Faster Than a Cheetah

Overcoming adversity is not always easy, especially when a setback is no one's fault. So how can you help your daughter whenever she hits a snag? How do you teach her to cope?

Next, I'll discuss seven pieces of wisdom you can use to teach your daughter how to overcome adversity.

I'll also introduce you to a couple of people whose life stories may be able to assist you when you speak to your daughter.

However, before I discuss any of that, let me introduce you to Sophia.

Sophia's story

Sophia, 18, lives in New Zealand with her brother, sister, mother, and father Mikal.

Like many 18-year-olds, Sophia wanted to go to college. She'd earned a high enough grade point average to get into her school of choice.

Plus, she was the kind of student who was normally accepted. So naturally she was accepted into the class of 2019. That was the good news.

Again like many young students who get into college, Sophia needed to pay for it. Like many families, hers fell into some financial trouble a few years ago during the Recession.

"Our savings, our home, everything got lost. We had no money to send her to university," her father Mikal shared, reflecting on his family's problems. If Sophia wanted to go to college, she'd have to pay for it herself.

For a young girl fresh out of high school, the thought of having to pay her own way was daunting. Paying for college can be a struggle.

Fortunately, however, Sophia was able to find a way.

According to her father, she feels blessed in some ways because paying her own tuition plus room and board have given her incredible strength and confidence that she may not have had otherwise.

Mikal has always been careful to raise his children to be "confident and responsible human beings, that can go out and function in life, without having to have their parents around, for the rest of their lives."

"She's out there," he said. "Luckily, she picked a university that's close to where we live. I see her once a week when I go into town. We catch up over coffee."

Sophia's prepared for the challenges of living on her own and paying for her college education. That's not easy, but she is meeting the challenge head-on.

Like many of us, she makes daily choices that affect her ability to pay for the things she needs.

For example, she may skip a movie with friends or meal at a restaurant to save money for essentials like groceries and rent. Every dollar saved add ups.

Here are Mikal's exact words:

"The total cost for this first year at university for Sophia is around $27,000 (about $19,000 U.S. dollars). She has been working in various jobs over the last 4 years, the main one being a check-out girl at a supermarket (she still works at a supermarket one evening a week to earn pocket money).

She had managed to save up a few 1,000 dollars this way, which was enough for her to pay the initial installment to the university.

As we have no money to support her, she was able to apply for grants and, being a good student, received a total of $6,000 ($4300 U.S.).

For the rest, which, fortunately, isn't a huge amount, she has got a student loan."

Watch this interview and discover more about Sophia and her dad as she reveals how she boosts self-confidence at http://authenticyou.tv/mikal-nielsen-8-replay/.

Your daughter may have to make similar choices when she grows up. My hope is that you will learn something about Sophia and her father Mikal that you can share with your daughter.

Think about what you can take away from Sophia's story to help you prepare your daughter to handle adversity.

Two more people who overcame adversity

Helen Keller – Nearly everyone has heard of Helen Keller. Over the years, Hollywood has made several films about her life.

Born in 1880, in Tuscumbia, Alabama, Keller contracted a severe illness before the age of two that took away her of her sight and hearing.

She struggled for many years in the world without sight or sound. But with the help of a teacher, she learned to communicate, despite her limitations.

Unfortunately, she never regained her senses. But she overcame adversity. Eventually, she graduated college, became an author and lecturer, and later cofounded the ACLU. She lived to be 87 years old.

Nick Vujicic – Nick overcame adversity, too. He is a husband, father, Christian evangelist, motivational speaker and author of Life without Limits. He also has no arms or legs.

In 1982, Nick was born in Melbourne, Australia, without limbs as a result of a rare condition called tetra-amelia syndrome.

Yet Nick has written numerous books and traveled around the world, lecturing to audiences about overcoming adversity.

There's so much to teach our young girls about overcoming adversity in the stories of Helen and Nick.

Thankfully, most girls won't have to face any obstacles that severe. But I'm confident they can learn something about facing adversity from these two people.

What about your daughter?

In the middle of a stressful situation, perhaps the last thing any daughter wants to hear is how dealing with adversity builds character. I should know. I've seen my daughters cover their ears when I try to tell them that.

While it may be true, that advice may not be the most helpful at that moment. Perhaps, a better approach might be to allow them time to relieve the stress— drawing, dancing, skipping rope, or whatever.

The point is: don't make things worse for your daughter. Don't dump more stress on to her stress. Stressful situations happen when she'll need your support and understanding the most.

When my daughters feel stressed out, I stay calm while acknowledging how they feel. When they see that I'm calm, they become calm.

Then, I give them some practical advice to help them deal with life's messes before they happen again.

8 Secrets To Helping Girls Overcome Adversity

In his book, The Success Principles, Jack Canfield talks about obstacles and the way to pass them by finding solutions that get around, over or through them.

Although your daughter may not have the same physical limitations as Helen Keller and Nick Vujicic, she will still need to learn how to get around, to overcome, and to go through obstacles life puts in her way.

1. Focus on the journey instead of the outcome.

This year, my daughter Daniella ran for student council president. She made four awesome posters, wrote an amazing campaign speech, rehearsed for hours, and presented her speech on stage in an auditorium filled with her peers. She was sensational.

Then she lost.

But what she gained was so much more important. After that campaign, she discovered she could write a speech. She realized she could stand in front of a crowd of hundreds and confidently speak in public.

She had fun, she made new friends, and now every sixth grader in school knows her name. More importantly, she didn't feel like she lost at all.

So the lesson here for your daughter is this: Sometimes the outcome is not what's important. What's important is what you gain along the way toward achieving your goal.

Encourage your daughter to not only do her best but also enjoy the process. She may win or lose, but, when she perseveres, she'll gain so much along the way.

2. Admit adversity is inevitable

There will be haters.

People and situations will position themselves between your daughter and her goals. What you need to do is prepare her for the inevitable. Let her know she'll have to persevere to get ahead or move to the next level.

One side note: You should also acknowledge that hard work doesn't always result in a win or success—and that's okay. The import thing is to try.

You'll also want to help her prepare in advance for whatever she wishes to do. Let her know that life does not always make things easy. She'll have to want it badly enough.

Because people often procrastinate, you'll want to encourage her to do the opposite.

Another benefit of preparation is that it improves performance. She'll perform better when she feels confident about whatever it is she's doing.

For example, my daughter realized early on that a victory in her school election was no longer guaranteed when the most popular boy in sixth grade, Mason, joined the race. I told her she'd have to work harder to beat him.

He was well-known and liked by many of the students. Yet Daniella became even more determined to win. As a relatively unknown candidate, she finished in second place in a very close race.

3. Support her.

Remind her of the real friends/family in her life. She needs to know who her support system is; she needs to know to whom she can go if a situation becomes too much for her to handle.

We assume they know to come to us but, you probably already know like most parents—sometimes you have to repeat what you say to your children to get them to listen.

Be prepared to do that this time, too. Except you'll want to tell her regularly before adversity strikes, so she'll remember immediately where to go.

Let her know that she can turn to your no matter what happens. Kids tend to clam up and forget they can confide in us.

4. Show her how you deal with adversity.

When my daughter was a toddler, she'd fall down and get back up like nothing even happened. Sometimes, she'd pause and look at me, waiting to see my reaction.

If I appeared worried or concerned about her, she'd start to cry. However, when I appeared undaunted, she'd get back up as if nothing ever happened.

Sometimes our children watch how we react to certain situations before they respond. They will model our behavior.

Your daughter will observe how you respond to setbacks and obstacles in your life. Show her the proper way to react in tough situations by setting a good example.

5. Let her know you've got her back.

One thing you can do, besides loving your daughter unconditionally, is to support her during troubling times.

Unfortunately, children often forget that we are there to help them even when they can't help themselves.

Therefore, you'll want to remind your daughter that she can come to you when she needs help.

6. Define failure.

Real failure happens when you never try in the first place. Although my daughter lost her election, she never felt like she failed because she tried something new and gave her best. She believed she gained so much from that experience.

In fact, as an unexpected consequence, she found success in other areas. With my guidance, she was able to identify her newly learned talents for speech writing and public speaking.

Plus she was able to recognize that the experience actually helped her mature as a person.

Your daughter will need you to help define her successes and failures as well. Tell her that she doesn't have to win every time to be successful. That's impossible.

Instead, teach her to discover the thing she's gained as a result of her efforts.

Be careful not to define every failure as a disappointing experience but as a learning one and guide her in articulating what she learned.

7. Find another way.

Because of their financial situation, Sophia's parents couldn't pay for her to attend college. Undaunted, she figured out a way to pay tuition and found a place to stay off-campus all on her own.

Hellen Keller couldn't hear or see. Yet with the help of others, she learned how to communicate and eventually graduated college.

Nick Vujicic was born without limbs. Yet he's written several books and lectures thousands of people every year. Did I mention he is also married and has a son?

When your daughter faces adversity, you have an opportunity to help her find another way to accomplish her dreams or reach her goals. Sometimes, there may only be one way.

But if you take the time to figure it out together, you may find an alternative solution, like Helen Keller and Nick Vujicic.

8. Believe that it's possible.

I've heard people say that if you believe it, then you can achieve it. That sounded like garbage at first, but then I thought about it.

For something to go your way, to win any sport or chess match or poker game or a video game or race, you have to believe that you can win.

You have to think that it is not only possible but also likely to happen.

One key point to remember: The next step will require lots and lots of hard work over an extended period of time. Success starts with belief and then hard work.

Furthermore, success is not guaranteed; however, failure is always guaranteed if you never try.

The lesson you need to instill in your daughter is this:

When you give up, when you stop believing you can achieve your dream, you lose.

Before she can achieve her dreams, she has to believe that her dreams are possible.

What to do now?

1) Give your daughter examples of people who face and overcome adversity.

2) Review the seven pieces of wisdom to prepare her to deal with adversity while she's young.

3) On the next page before chapter eight, read my interview with Mikal who shares his tips to help you boost your daughter's self-esteem.

4) Download your PDF of the seven secrets to helping your daughter overcome adversity at www.raisingyourdaughter.com/adversity.

What's next?

In this chapter, I discussed how to overcome adversity and I gave you examples of people who have fought through adversity and won.

In chapter eight, I will reveal to you my other reason for writing this book. But first, read the excerpt of my interview with New Zealander, Mikal, on the next page where he reveals his most important advice yet.

Fatherly Advice

Born in Denmark, Mikal is an author and life coach who lives in New Zealand with his wife and three children—two girls and one boy. During my conversation with him, I gathered several key pieces of advice that I'd like to share with you.

Read my interview with Mikal Nielsen, author of The Quick Fix to Any Problem.

What have you taught your daughters about life, and how have you prepared them for the future?

There are a few core principles. First, let them create their own experiences. You can't do that for them. Wisdom doesn't come from knowledge, it comes from experiences.

Also, teach them responsibility, even though they get pissed off a lot when they have to clean the house, wash the dishes or do things with the family.

My wife and I keep emphasizing that because that's how life is after mom and dad. For me, it's all about responsibility—taking full responsibility for yourself, your actions, and your future. If I could put it all into one thing, that would be it.

Also, I've made it very clear to my girls that I don't understand everything they go through. I'm not pretending that I do.

I'm very honest about what I know, and what I don't know. I'm very happy to say, "I haven't got a clue," rather than pretend to be the one who knows it all.

Sometimes, we think our children don't listen to us. So, how do you get your daughters to listen to you?

I think the truth is slightly different. I think the truth is our children always listen. They don't always do what we say, but they always listen.

They'll remember something you said six years ago, and they'll remind you if what you do doesn't stack up somehow.

You say to them, "Don't smoke." Then, they see you smoking. They're going to follow what you've done, more often than what you've said.

My wife and I believe that we should behave the way we want our kids to behave. Rather than tell them what to do, we show them.

We're not perfect parents, so it doesn't always work, but we do our best.

What other advice can you give to dads who are raising daughters?

I think what a lot of dad's miss out on is taking the opportunity to include their girls in what they like to do. Not so much taking her to work, but inviting her into your world.

For me, I love cafes. I take my girls along with me because that's my scene. If we go out, we're not going swimming because that's not me.

I'm not a nature boy going into the bush. I'm going to take them to a cafe. We'll sit down and have a hot chocolate or get something to eat. We connect in that sense because that's my place.

Daughters need to know about your world. It's not something that should be a secret.

If you're a doctor, show them your work. If you're passionate about some sport, then involve them; show them.

Why dads should know the hidden reason why I wrote this book. Turn the page to find out.

CHAPTER 9

One Last Thing You Should
Know to Help Your Daughter

I have a confession to make. I told you this book would
tell you how to boost your daughter's self-esteem, self-
image, and self-respect.

Of course, that's true. I kept my promise. But, I didn't
reveal everything. That is until now. This book isn't
just about your daughter. It's about you, too.

If you've learned nothing else from this book, I want
you to remember that your daughter will copy what
you do.

Yes, they will obey you and do what you say ... to a
point. At the end of the day, they will copy you, and

when they get older, they'll seek out men who treat them the same way you've treated them.

That's why it's important that while you're boosting your daughter's self-esteem and teaching her things she needs to know, you're also setting a great example.

Ask yourself: "How am I handling responsibility, respecting others, and overcoming adversity? What examples am I setting for my little girl to follow?"

So while it's important that we start teaching our girls how to behave and handle themselves as they mature, it's just as important that we practice what we preach.

I've heard someone say that, "Imitation is the best form of flattery." What do our daughters see when they imitate us?

If we want to improve our daughters' lives, we have to start by improving ourselves. That's not to say we are broken and that we need to be fixed to be great parents.

We just need to understand that what our children see us do and hear us say will have as great an impact on their lives as what we tell them.

If you want to improve the life of your daughter and prepare her for a brighter future, show her what that looks like.

Show her by practicing the lessons you teach her. Gandhi is credited with the saying, "Be the change you want to see in the world."

As you think about those words, remember two things:

It's not what you say; it's how you say it.

Watch how you speak to your daughter because she will expect everyone to speak to her the same way you do.

When she grows up, she will attract others who will treat her the way you treat her because she will equate love with however you have expressed it through your words, tone of voice, and actions to her.

Think about it. Your child feels loved by you. But what if you speak to her harshly, criticize and yell at her? Just think about who will come into her life when she gets older.

She may become attracted to other men who yell and criticize her, too, because that's the way she received love from you.

Of course, you don't want that to happen. You want what's best for her, right? That's why it's important to watch how you express yourself to your daughter.

You will make mistakes.

You can do this. However, you're going to make mistakes every day—some big and some small. That's okay. It's normal.

But when you make a mistake, take responsibility, apologize and move on from there. Believe me, it will work wonders for your relationship.

This may be hard for some. Apologizing makes you feel vulnerable and fallible.

So what?

It's not easy to admit you're wrong especially when you are the parent. But it really does help make things better.

Give it a shot. See what happens. Try everything I've suggested in this book. Use it to boost your daughter's self-esteem.

Strengthen the bond you have with your daughter.

I hope that because of what you've read, you'll be able to help your daughter for years to come.

Good luck.

Keep investing in your daughter's future.

She'll be glad you did. And so will you.

BEFORE YOU GO...

Review This Book

I'd like to say ...

Thank you for reading this book.

I sincerely hope you've found something useful, and I hope my book will be of great benefit to you and your daughter. But, it would be a shame if you didn't tell someone else about it.

So, tell the world what you think.

Sign in to Amazon first (if necessary) and leave your honest review at:

www.amazon.com/product-reviews/B00YUUWW34/

DEDICATIONS

This book is dedicated to my wife and daughters. They have been putting up with my late nights and long hours as I've been writing this book. I appreciate their patience and support.

ACKNOWLEDGEMENTS

This book is possible because of so many people who have helped me along the way. Thank you, Jesus, family and friends.

I'd also like to thank Chandler Bolt, Chelsea Miller, Steve Windsor, Nick Loper, Nick Stephenson, Tom Corson-Knowles, David Wood, Krista Brubaker, Marie Bailey, Mikal Nielsen and, the best editor in the world, Nancy Pile.

For the writing lessons, I'd like to thank Kevin Rogers, Jon Morrow, Lysa Terkeurst, Jyotsna Ramachandra, Steve Scott, Henneke Duistermaan, Ian Brodie, Akash Karia, John Tighe, Carol Tice, Linda Formichelli, Mary Jaksch, Danny Iny, Ryan Levesque, Lysa Terkeurst, Steve Windsor, Tim Grahl, Pat Flynn, Jeff Goins, K.M. Weiland, Kelsye Nelson, Joseph Michael, Rene Swope, Kevin Rogers, Demian Farnworth, Chip & Dan Health, and Nancy Duarte, Noah Kagan, Russell Brunson, Derek Doepker and

Derek Halpren. These are people I admire, and I'm thankful I've found them online.

For inspiration and motivation, I'd like to acknowledge Lynn Cowell, Rachel Wojnarowsk (a.k.a, Rachel Wojo), Michael Hyatt, Gavin Wainwright Sr., Angela Wainwright, Darryle Foy, Cynthia Foy, M.D. Stokes, E. Wayne Hines, David Downey, Jillian Downey, Meg Meeker, Brook Lynn, Bruce Van Horn, Jon Acuff, Joel Osteen, T.D. Jakes, Joyce Meyer, Lynn Mosher, Max Lucado, Nathan Barry, Brian Harris, Komanzi Constable, Matt Stone, Brian Clark, Kristen Eckstein, Brene Brown and Nancy Pyle.

ABOUT THE AUTHOR

After meeting his wife in the military, Michael struggled to find his purpose, moving every few years with his family, living in North America, Europe and Asia. Luckily, he found his passion for parenting, writing and helping others. When he's not working, he's writing about parenting, self-publishing, and faith. If he's not falling asleep at his laptop, you'll find him hanging out with his kids or watching football on TV. At some point along the way, he managed to earn a bachelor's degree in communication studies from the University of Maryland University College, too.

Email him at: michael@faithwritings.com.

Twitter: www.twitter.com/faithwritings

Facebook: www.facebook.com/raisingyourdaughter

RECOMMENDED READING

Strong Fathers, Strong Daughters by Meg Meeker

The Success Principles by Jack Canfield

Life without Limits: Inspiration for a Ridiculously Good Life by Nick Vujicic

The 5 Love Languages of Children by Gary D. Chapman

The Five Love Languages of Teenagers by Gary D. Chapman

REFERENCES

1) Elovson, A. (n.d.). Secretly Sad: Overcoming Gender Disappointment. Retrieved from http://www.babble.com/pregnancy/overcoming-gender-disappointment/2/

2) Babauta, L. (n.d.). 25 Killer Actions to Boost Your Self-Confidence. Retrieved from http://zenhabits.net/25-killer-actions-to-boost-your-self-confidence/

3) Babauta, L. (n.d.). 25 Killer Actions to Boost Your Self-Confidence. Retrieved from http://zenhabits.net/25-killer-actions-to-boost-your-self-confidence/

4) Moore, A. (n.d.). Top 10 ways to show confidence with body language. Retrieved from http://www.askmen.com/grooming/project/top-10-ways-to-show-confidence-with-body-language_7.html

5) Blumen, L. (2013). Teaching kids self-respect early is crucial. Retrieved from http://tvoparents.tvo.org/blog/tvoparents-blog/teaching-kids-self-respect-early-crucial

6) VanClay, M. (n.d.). The caring child: How to teach empathy. Retrieved from http://www.babycenter.com/0_the-caring-child-how-to-teach-empathy_67146.bc

7) Dewar, G. (2014). Teaching empathy: Evidence-based tips for fostering empathy in children. Retrieved from http://www.parentingscience.com/teaching-empathy-tips.html

8) Dewar, G. (2014). Teaching empathy: Evidence-based tips for fostering empathy in children. Retrieved from http://www.parentingscience.com/teaching-empathy-tips.html

9) Page, A. (n.d.). 10 Warning signs that you have low self-confidence. Retrieved from http://www.lifehack.org/articles/communication/10-warning-signs-that-you-have-low-self-confidence.html

10) Ettus, S. (2012). 8 essential steps to raising confident girls. Retrieved from http://www.forbes.com/sites/samanthaettus/2012/10/11/8-essential-steps-to-raising-confident-girls/

Additional References

Fiorentino, A. (2015). Baseball legend Curt Schilling defends his daughter in the best way. Retrieved from http://www.womansday.com/relationships/family-friends/a40439/baseball-legend-curt-schilling-defends-his-daughter-in-the-best-way-possible/

Kasdan, M. (2015). Internet trolling explained? Enough is enough. Time to tell their mommies. Retrieved from http://goodmenproject.com/featured-content/sports-explained-trolls-mkdn/

Parent, J. (2014). To the boys who may one day date my daughter. Retrieved from https://www.youtube.com/watch?v=KcIwZ1Dth0c

CBS Sunday Morning. (2015). Minnesota basketball team loses a losing record. Retrieved from https://www.youtube.com/watch?v=Ivkhgr9vivo.

A Father's Guide to Raising Daughters

How to Boost Her Self-Esteem, Self-Image and Self-Respect

Made in the USA
Middletown, DE
05 May 2017